Too Cute!

Baby Rhinos

by Rachael Barnes

BELLWETHER MEDIA
MINNEAPOLIS, MN

BLASTOFF!
Beginners

Blastoff! Beginners are developed by literacy experts and educators to meet the needs of early readers. These engaging informational texts support young children as they begin reading about their world. Through simple language and high frequency words paired with crisp, colorful photos, Blastoff! Beginners launch young readers into the universe of independent reading.

BLASTOFF! DISCOVERY

BLASTOFF! READERS

BLASTOFF! Beginners

Blastoff! Universe

Reading Level

Grade K

Grades 1-3

Grade 4

Sight Words in This Book 🔍

a	have	of	them
are	he	one	they
at	in	play	this
big	is	she	to
eat	it	the	two
get	look	their	will

This edition first published in 2023 by Bellwether Media, Inc.

No part of this publication may be reproduced in whole or in part without written permission of the publisher. For information regarding permission, write to Bellwether Media, Inc., Attention: Permissions Department, 6012 Blue Circle Drive, Minnetonka, MN 55343.

Library of Congress Cataloging-in-Publication Data
Names: Barnes, Rachael, author.
Title: Baby rhinos / by Rachael Barnes.
Description: Minneapolis, MN : Bellwether Media, Inc., 2023. | Series: Blastoff! beginners: Too cute! | Includes bibliographical references and index. | Audience: Ages 4-7 | Audience: Grades K-1
Identifiers: LCCN 2022036385 (print) | LCCN 2022036386 (ebook) | ISBN 9798886871111 (library binding) | ISBN 9798886871999 (paperback) | ISBN 9798886872378 (ebook)
Subjects: LCSH: Rhinoceroses--Infancy--Juvenile literature.
Classification: LCC QL737.U63 B367 2023 (print) | LCC QL737.U63 (ebook) | DDC 599.66/81392--dc23/eng/20220729
LC record available at https://lccn.loc.gov/2022036385
LC ebook record available at https://lccn.loc.gov/2022036386

Editor: Betsy Rathburn   Designer: Jeffrey Kollock

Printed in the United States of America, North Mankato, MN.

Table of Contents

A Baby Rhino!   4

Life with Mom   6

Growing Up!   18

Baby Rhino Facts   22

Glossary   23

To Learn More   24

Index   24

A Baby Rhino!

Look at the
baby rhino.
Hello, calf!

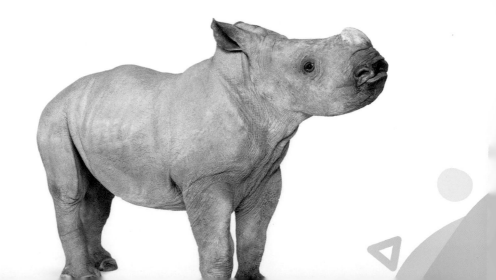

Life with Mom

Calves are
big babies!
They have
wrinkly skin.

wrinkly skin

Calves stay
close to mom.
She keeps
them safe.

mom

Calves drink
mom's milk.
They eat plants.

They roll
in mud.
It keeps
them cool.

They **stomp** their feet to play. They learn to **charge**!

Calves get
sleepy fast.
They take a lot
of naps.

Growing Up!

Calves get huge!
They grow one
or two horns.

horn

This calf is three.
Soon he will
leave mom.
Bye, calf!

Baby Rhino Facts

Rhino Life Stages

calf   adult

A Day in the Life

drink mom's   play   nap
milk

Glossary

charge

to run at
something or
someone

stomp

to hit feet hard
on the ground

wrinkly

having a lot of
small folds

To Learn More

ON THE WEB

FACTSURFER

Factsurfer.com gives you a safe, fun way to find more information.

1. Go to www.factsurfer.com.

2. Enter "baby rhinos" into the search box and click 🔍.

3. Select your book cover to see a list of related content.

Index

big, 6
charge, 14
cool, 12
drink, 10
eat, 10
feet, 14
grow, 18
horns, 18, 19
huge, 18

learn, 14
milk, 10
mom, 8, 9, 10, 20
mud, 12
naps, 16
plants, 10
play, 14
rhino, 4

roll, 12
safe, 8
skin, 6, 7
sleepy, 16
stomp, 14